about this particular place and held it in high regard. Spear points fashioned from Alibates flint could cut deeply into the flesh of edible animals. The same flint shaped into scrapers, knives, and hammers was more durable than similar tools made out of bone, wood, or shell.

The flint the local people didn't use they traded to other people for items brought from long distances away—shells from the Pacific coast, dried fish from the Gulf of Mexico, malleable red pipestone from Minnesota, animal furs from the Rocky Mountains. But few gifts matched the importance of the smooth, workable flint found at this location. Six thousand years before the invention of the wheel, seven thousand years before the construction of the Great Pyramids in Egypt, nine thousand years before the Roman Empire, ten thousand years before the birth of Christ, Paleo-Americans living in North America sculpted chunks of smooth, variegated flint into serviceable tools and weapon points which enabled them not only to survive but to live more comfortably.

Alibates Flint Quarries National Monument is located in the heart of the Texas Panhandle. The Panhandle is part of the Great Plains ecosystem, which originally comprised thousands of square miles of grasslands stretching east of the Rocky Mountains, south to the Rio Grande, north into Canada. The earth layers composing this immense land mass lie upon a marine rock sheet which emerged with the upthrust of the ancestral Rocky Mountains some 100 million years ago. The tall peaks attracted rainclouds, which deluged the range, forming wide rivers that charged east, eroding the mountains, carrying masses of rock and sand down onto the rock sheet. Between 20 and 30 million years ago, the gradient leveled off and the moisture slackened. Streams fanned out, pooling into vast expanses of shallow water. Bits and flecks of debris twirled to the bottom, piling up reefs and bars that choked off the current. But water, being water, sought new outlets; eventually, over the eons, this massive deposition, known as the Ogallala Formation, formed a complex network of interlacing channels that sloped generally eastward across an eroded alluvial plain.

So where does the flint come from? Long before the creation of the Rocky Mountains or the Ogallala Formation, a deposit of clay and limestone, called dolomite, was laid down during the Permian Age, some 260 to 280 million years ago. This dolomite is laced with generous nodules and seams of colorful flint, which formed when mineral-bearing water seeped into the layer, replacing it with a hard, fine-grained quartz. (Petrified wood is formed in a similar manner.) The light-gray dolomite capstone at the surface of Alibates Flint Quarries National

Grass blowing in wind

Primrose

Alibates flint arrow points

Monument literally bulges with flint outcroppings. The panoply of bright colors (red, yellow, purple, gray, white) banding the flint distinguishes it from most other flint on the continent.

The Panhandle is a land of variable climate. The wind is a constant factor. Few trees or declivities impede its flow. It sweeps and saws incessantly, drawing the moisture from the grass, chapping the skin on the face. Winter "northers" can gust up to 60 to 80 miles per hour. Spring and summer bring thunderstorms that drench the earth with short bursts; annual rainfall averages 21 inches. The intense runoff gushes through the gullies and canyons around the Canadian River "breaks." Elsewhere, there are few outlets, and the water collects in shallow playas until it evaporates or percolates down through the sand, clay, and limerock into aquifers. In the volatile atmosphere of spring and early summer, tornadoes churn across the level terrain. The summer heat, though low on humidity, can be searingly hot.

The relentless sun and burning winds nurture a shortgrass habitat: little and big bluestem, blue grama, and buffalo grass. Classic bison-grazing turf, and before that, ten thousand years ago, when the climate was cooler and wetter, food for the Columbian mammoths and other grass-eating behemoths that once roamed this part of the world.

The draws near the Canadian River shelter stands of cottonwoods, willows, mesquite, one-seed juniper, catclaw, and chinaberry. Each spring, wildflowers—fringed puccoon, fleabane daisy, woolly loco, blue gilia—blossom into riotous color. Late May and early June is the optimum time to view the flora in full bloom.

The big animals are long gone from a land that once nourished a considerable variety of them. It's hard to imagine these creatures slogging across a cool, wet grassland, marking the mud around the many marshes with their distinctive prints. In addition to the mammoths, there were giant sloths, diminutive horses, two-toed camels, massive turtles, and ancient bison (bigger than the ones we know, heavier, shaggier, with long, curved horns). The fauna surviving today seems puny by comparison: coyote, badger, pronghorn, cougar, whitetail deer, mule deer, raccoon, porcupine, striped skunk. A hundred and fifty years ago there were gray wolves, grizzly and black bears, bison too numerous to count… all gone now.

Eleven thousand years ago the climate of the Texas Panhandle was cooler and wetter than it is today. It was the close of the last Ice Age, and far to the north the huge glaciers that had covered much of the northern half of the continent were in full retreat. Large, shambling, grass-eating animals roamed the

North American plains, stalked by hunters bearing long spears, many tipped with slim, deadly, agate-colored points mined from quarries located in present-day Alibates Flint Quarries National Monument.

Over a period of several thousand years the quantity and variety of these huge creatures diminished. Climate changes contributed to their demise, along with the deadly efficiency of Paleo-Americans armed with exquisitely crafted spear points. This era has been called "the time of great dying," and when it ended around six thousand years ago many of the big, warm-blooded, lactating animals that once dominated the interior flatlands were gone.

The early hunters were surprisingly mobile, carrying their entire material culture on their backs. They gathered plants, roots, and seeds, which they supplemented with meat from the many creatures roaming the grasslands. The best hunters were adept at driving the big animals into a marsh or wetlands, where they assailed them on all sides with spears. The mammoths reared and trumpeted, flailing with their feet and tusks, no doubt wounding many of the hunters. Spear points embedded in the animals' skeletons, later unearthed by archeologists at sites in New Mexico and the Texas Panhandle, offer valuable clues into stone-age technology. Two of

the earliest types of points were named Clovis and Folsom. These points—frequently crafted from Alibates flint and designed to penetrate all the way to the animals' vitals—were slim, tapered, and exceedingly sharp.

Between six thousand and two thousand years ago, following the Big Game Hunters in the Texas Panhandle, a tradition called the Plains Archaic evolved slowly but significantly. The people of this culture subsisted on a combination of hunting and gathering. In caves south of Kenton, Oklahoma, archeologists uncovered refuse heaps containing the bones of bison, deer, pronghorn, rabbit, and other animals, as well as the remains of vegetal items such as acorns, wild seeds, maize (corn), and squash. The Plains Village Culture, which developed at Alibates about A.D. 1000 and ended around 1500, was characterized by a more settled way of life; while hunting continued to be important, the cultivation of maize, beans, and squash became widespread.

Among the most important people to occupy the area of the Alibates flint quarries were those who flourished during the Antelope Creek Phase of the Plains Village Culture, between A.D. 1200 and 1450. (Their potsherds and other artifacts help determine these dates.) Archeologists first thought the Antelope Creek villagers were a Puebloan people, with cultural and racial ties to native cultures living to the west along the Rio Grande. Subsequent study indicates that they were a pottery-making people who developed from those already in the area. They settled along the bluffs and tributaries of the Canadian River, where they displayed a considerably more complex culture than their predecessors.

Architecture is the Antelope Creek people's most remarkable achievement. They often located their villages on high ground overlooking the Canadian River and its tributaries. The remains of two of these villages can be seen today within Alibates Flint Quarries National Monument. The remains feature substantial blocks of single-story rooms, variously shaped and sized, made of stone masonry linked together in a contiguous line similar to the Pueblo architecture to the west. Stone slabs placed vertically in parallel rows formed the walls or provided supports for walls made of brush; the spaces between the parallel walls were packed with adobe mud to insulate the dwellings from excessive cold and heat. (How ancient people built their homes, the layout and materials they used, convey important clues as to who they were and what they thought.)

Some of these people built their dwellings within walking distance of the flint quarries, which they apparently worked with some regularity, digging under the surface to unearth the higher quality chert. They, or their predecessors, also pecked out petroglyphs on the rounded crests of dolomite capstone—images of turtles and bison, along with several outsized human feet, mysterious representations the meanings of which we can only ponder.

The Antelope Creek people grew corn, beans, and squash. They hunted deer, pronghorn, and bison. An important agricultural implement was the bison scapula (shoulder blade) hoe. Their pottery was decorated with a rough cord-marked pattern. Their chief weapon was the bow and arrow, the arrows tipped by points made from the same bright, deadly stone used by their Folsom and Clovis predecessors.

In 1541 Spanish conquistador Francisco Vazquez de Coronado passed through the region in search

Cord-marked ceramic vessel

of the mythical kingdom of Quivira. During his long march into the grassy interior, which took him across the Texas Panhandle, parts of Oklahoma, and into Kansas, Coronado encountered a people, probably Plains Apaches—Athabaskans, originally from northwest Canada.

The horses the Spaniards introduced to the region profoundly affected the lives of the native people. With the horse, Indians were able to cover greater distances, carry more equipment, hunt bison—known as buffalo—in a more productive fashion. The horse also created a warrior caste whose prowess and daring were to bedevil Spanish, Mexican, and American authorities for two centuries.

In the early 1700s, the Plains Apaches were displaced from the Texas Panhandle by the Comanches, a tribe originally from the Great Basin. The Comanche were one of the first tribes to acquire horses from the Spanish; possessed of a fluid mobility, armed with flintlock rifles and pistols purchased from French traders, they transformed themselves into a loose, confederated band of ferocious raiders. Around 1790, they allied themselves with the Kiowa; together, the two tribes dominated the Southern Plains.

Traders known as comancheros, operating out of Santa Fe and Chihuahua City, traded guns and ammunition to the Indians for buffalo hides. Arrows remained an integral part of the Indian armory, and until manufactured steel arrow tips fully replaced those crafted of flint (sometime in the 1870s), people continued to journey to the Alibates quarries.

With the exception of the comanchero traders and ciboleros (Hispanic buffalo hunters), few people of Spanish origin ventured into the unknown interior of the Texas Panhandle. In the 1840s and 50s, several American expeditions from Missouri and Arkansas skirted the region looking for swifter and safer routes to the markets at Santa Fe and Chihuahua City. Until the 1870s, the terrain, immense and poorly mapped, remained mostly uninhabited, a refuge for raiding cultures, a place where they could hunt buffalo, fatten up their weary horses, and hide out from their enemies.

Anglo pioneers trickling into the Texas frontier in the 1840s and 1850s exacerbated relations with the Indians, compelling them to strike back in fury. At the close of the U.S.-Mexican War in 1848, with Texas formally transferred to the control of the United States, the U.S. Army constructed a series of forts that slowly and inexorably drew a tight ring around the traditional Panhandle hunting grounds of the Indians.

In response to the demand for buffalo hides back east following

Old excavating photos 1930s

9

Dolomite caprock

crunch came in September when a force led by Col. Ranald Mackenzie surprised a Comanche, Kiowa, and Cheyenne encampment deep inside Palo Duro Canyon, south of present-day Amarillo. The troopers slipped undetected down the steep slopes and attacked at dawn, routing the Indians and burning their tipis, food supply, and buffalo robes. On Mackenzie's orders, the soldiers then shot some 1,100 horses, depriving the Comanche and their allies of their mobility and wealth. The attack broke the back of Indian resistance in the Panhandle; the following year, the army settled warring bands of Comanche and Kiowa in what is now western Oklahoma.

the Civil War, hunters fanned out over the Southern Plains, slaughtering every herd they could find. The overhunting of this invaluable animal outraged the Indians, and they fought back fiercely to preserve their way of life. In 1874, a conflict known as the Red River War erupted, involving Kiowa, Comanche, and other plains tribes harried by cavalry probes that penetrated deeper into the formerly safe haven of the Texas Panhandle. There were raids and counterraids, several pitched battles, most notably on June 27, 1874, at a place called Adobe Walls along the Canadian River, a few miles northeast of Alibates Flint Quarries National Monument. The final

WITH THE INDIANS REMOVED and the great bison herds decimated, the Panhandle was briefly, in the words of historian Frederick W. Rathjen, "a cartographic void." But not for long. Former comancheros brought thousands of sheep from New Mexico and set them out to graze on the nutritious shortgrass along the Canadian River. These pastores immediately ran afoul of Anglo cattlemen such as Charles Goodnight and T.S. Bugbee.

But for the moment the Panhandle was big enough to accommodate all newcomers. Goodnight eventually abandoned his claims along the Canadian to the sheep-

Prehistoric petroglyph

Chinaberry tree

The trail to Alibates Flint Quarries

men and moved his operation into the depths of Palo Duro Canyon, where he and John Adair established the famous JA Ranch. Bugbee, a Yankee from Maine, established the Quarter Circle T Ranch in Hutchinson County, in what is now Lake Meredith National Recreation Area. Significantly, the first thing Goodnight did was hire a team of men to kill off most of the remaining buffalo. The cities of America were filling up, and the demand for fresh beef meant big profits for enterprising cattlemen. The future of the West held no place for the once mighty bison.

Growth and development came slowly to the wide-open spaces of the Texas Panhandle. The first federal census taken in 1880 tallied a mere 1,607 residents, many of whom were either ranchers or sheep herders. Amarillo, destined to become the region's major city, was known as "Ragtown" after the cattle hides that provided shelter for the majority of its citizens. Even today the Panhandle population remains scanty—less than half a million.

In 1887 the Santa Fe and the Fort Worth and Denver City Railroad reached the Panhandle. The great cattle drives, so much a part of western lore, sputtered out as more and more beeves were shipped back east by rail. Panhandle settlement accelerated. Little towns, some no more than a crude hut

or two, sprouted like mushrooms alongside the tracks. Several of the bigger ranches were broken up and parceled out in smaller tracts to new settlers. Dryland farming on a limited scale was practiced until hydrologists tapped into the Ogallala aquifer in the 1940s, which resulted in intensive irrigation and vastly improved crop yields.

In 1918 the first natural gas well in the Panhandle was drilled near the Canadian River. Three years later, an oil gusher erupted near the town of Borger, 12 miles northeast of Alibates Flint Quarries National Monument. The rush was on. The population of Borger boomed within a matter of weeks to around 18,000. Claims were established, derricks thrown up, and sharp drills chewed through the earth. The stench of sulfur and oil soon replaced the scent of the warm grassy winds that had blown over the region for centuries.

Nearby Lake Meredith, a project of the Bureau of Reclamation in conjunction with eleven local municipalities, was impounded in 1965 by the earth-filled Sanford Dam on the Canadian River north of the town of Fritch. The purpose was to establish a stable water supply for the Panhandle population. That same year, Congress designated Alibates a national monument. It was named after Alibates creek, which was originally named for Allen "Allie" Bates, a cowboy who lived on a ranch near the quarries in the late nineteenth century. The monument is relatively undeveloped. Park rangers lead guided walking tours of the quarries on a schedule that varies with the seasons.

Compared to what it was in the nineteenth century, the Panhandle seems sleepy today—a ranching, agricultural, and oil emporium, fully tamed and subdued, a mere shadow of its former rough-and-tumble self. But despite all the additions and improvements, there's still something ineffable about the place. Maybe it's the enormity of the sky, the way it seems to soar beyond the boundary of the horizon, the way nothing seems to stand between you and the edge of the world.

ALIBATES FLINT QUARRIES National Monument is about flint-working. Flint-knapping demonstrations are done upon request, when a volunteer with that special skill is available.

Flintknappers are an odd sort. They like to work with stone. They like the way it feels in their hands. They like the sound the flint makes when properly struck with a hammerstone. They like to watch the flakes peel off in uniform layers.

Stonemaking may be humankind's first art form. Knapping means "to break with a sharp blow." The act consists of two separate functions. The first is percussive, that is, striking flakes from a hard core to form a rudimentary shape. The second is reductive, or refining the shape by pressing away small pieces with a soft hammer tool called a billet, usually the tip of a deer, moose, or elk antler.

Flint is a form of chert. When properly struck, its crystalline structure reacts like a fluid, making a conchoidal fracture that splinters in a predictable manner.

Paleo-Americans sometimes heated the stones they intended to shape to make them flake more easily. They buried the stones in sand between layers of smoldering coal and warmed them to around 500 degrees Fahrenheit to make them more tractable. Once the stone cooled, they could work it more easily.

Paul Hellweg, a modern flint-knapper and author of a book on the subject, feels that to obtain the best results flintknappers must form a visual image of each flake they intend to knock off the original core. They must picture it in their minds, and if the piece that flakes off approximates their imaginative rendering, then they must be doing it right.

The blow is often struck with a hard, round rock, usually a river cobble. This rock is harder than the chert core, and the blow must be delivered with great precision and skill.

The technique of flintknapping has hardly changed in 12,000 years.

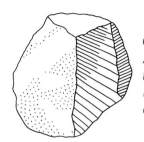

Chunk of Alibates bedrock known as a "core"

Roughout

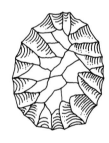

Trade blank

Preform

Spear point

13

Scattered flint

goggles and keeping antiseptic and bandages close by.

A thousand years ago, Plains Villagers built their homes fairly close to the site of a quarry. Cores are heavy and clunky, and the knappers usually spent their day reducing them in size so they could carry them back to their houses and finish them off there. In addition, quarries were sometimes regarded as holy sites, and most likely some ceremony was performed before the knappers commenced their daily labor. Even today, thousands of years after they were first fashioned, Clovis and Folsom spear points, with their lanceolate shapes, conspicuous flutes, and sharp edges, emit a special look and feeling. What mix of technical know-how and aesthetic sense these crafts people brought to bear on the project we will never know exactly. They left no written record, and regarding the rituals that accompanied their labor we can only speculate. But we do know that for native people the spiritual

Posture is important; the knapper needs to be squarely settled on a sturdy rock or tree stump, with the core clutched in his or her palm and braced tightly between the knees. The knapper then carefully buffs off the sharp edges to make the core easier to grip. After that, the actual shaping begins. With swift, precise strokes delivered with the round cobble the knapper reduces the core to a rough outline of the finished product. The knapper then sculpts and smooths the product with the tip of a deer tine or other tool.

Flint can be hazardous to work with. The slivers can be acutely sharp, and no doubt ancient knappers occasionally lost fingers and even their eyesight to popping flakes. Modern knappers have the option of wearing protective

Black-tailed jackrabbit